1000 SUBSCRIBERS IN 30 DAYS

ANURADHA SRIVASTAVA

1,000SUBSCRIBERS IN 30 DAYS

Proven List Building Methods

The #1 1000 Subscribers in 30 Days Free Training That Will Sky Rocket Affiliate Commissions Online

CLICK HERE TO RESERVE YOUR SEAT

Hit this blue line to apply.

We've all heard the saying that the "money is in the list", but how many of us are actively building our email list? From my experience online I have come to realize that while most of us understand the need for a subscriber list, most people are not sure how to go about setting one up and building it.

That's what this report will try to solve, the problem of not knowing where to start and where to go to start getting subscribers on your new list. As you will soon read, getting to 1,000 subscribers in 30 days is a very reasonable goal, you will just need to focus on certain steps and take action. So let's get started!

Step #1: Funnel Creation

The first step before you can start building an email list is that you will need to create a few web pages in order to send traffic to, which then allows the visitors to actually sign up to your list. There are a few pages that you will need; you first need a squeeze page, then a one-time offer page, as well as a down-sell page for that one-time offer.

Let me quickly explain what each of those pages are and why you need them. The squeeze page is the email capture page, where you will need to put your autoresponder opt-in form code on so that visitors can sign up to your list. This is the most important page that you will need. All other pages are optional, but still highly recommended.

The one-time offer page is the page that viewers will see and be redirected to as soon as they fill in your opt-in form. This page hosts a low priced offer, usually within the $10-

$20 range, which helps you to recoup costs that you might incur when purchasing traffic.

Then the down-sell offer page is similar to the one-time offer, but instead, it is a very low cost offer which visitors will see if they do not purchase the one-time offer.

If you want to get really complicated, but at the same time make a lot more money, you can keep adding offer pages to your funnel. For example, you could have an upsell page for a mid-high ticket product, then also backend offers as well. But for starters I would recommend at least having those three pages, the squeeze page, one-time offer, and a down-sell page.

Squeeze Page:

Let's get into the very important squeeze page. I'm sure you are familiar with internet marketing related squeeze pages, they generally all look the same, and that's not a good thing. Internet marketers tend to copy one another quite regularly. They see a page which they think is working well, then they copy it, then someone else does the same thing. Before you know it, that page is no longer converting well anymore because too many people are promoting the same page, everyone is seeing the same pages over and over again.

When creating your squeeze page, make it as unique as you can. The more it's different from other pages and the more it stands out, the better it will convert for you.

When creating a squeeze page I have found that very simple pages work the best, pages which have a big headline, a short sub-headline, and the opt-in form, nothing much else on the page. Keeping it simple and to the point helps to boost conversion rates.

You will also want to only have an email address field for visitors to fill in. By default most opt-in forms have a name and email field, but requiring a name only lowers conversion rates. That's not to say that you can't use the name field, but just be aware that your conversions will be lower with it.

So what is a good conversion rate for a squeeze page? The higher you can have it, the better it is. But overall, I aim for at least 40% conversions. That means that if I had 100 visitors to the squeeze page, 40 of them will subscribe to my list. I've had higher than that, over 50%, but I start out aiming for 40%. Then I keep testing and tweaking the page until I get the highest conversions that I can.

To create a squeeze page (or any of the other pages as well), you can use a variety of programs to help you do it. If you are comfortable creating a web page from scratch, then by all means do that. But if you are not familiar with how to do that then I would suggest using a combination of WordPress and OptimizePress. WordPress in general helps to create web pages very quickly, but it is limited in how much you can easily customize a page. OptimizePress is a plug-in for WordPress which makes creating squeeze pages and offer pages very easy. It allows you to quickly create and then edit pages at any time, you can easily add-in your autoresponder form code into a page.

Hit this blue line to apply.

Free Gift:

One thing that you will need in conjunction with your squeeze page is some kind of free gift or free offer to entice visitors to sign up to your list. This can be a simple PDF report, a few videos, or anything that is on a hot topic within your niche.

Once you know what your free offer is, you can then write your squeeze page headline to tell your visitors what it is that they will be receiving once they fill in the opt-in form.

Once they do join your list you can then deliver the free gift to them though your autoresponder follow-up email series which I will explain about in the next chapter.

One important note about this free gift is that it should be of good quality. Don't use a report that was written five years ago with content which isn't relevant anymore. Also don't use a gift which is already been given away by hundreds of other people. You will want it to be as unique as possible so that your subscribers will enjoy it and be able to use the information is provides. This is important if you want to build up trust with your subscribers.

One-Time Offer Page:

Now that you have a squeeze page with a free offer, it's time to consider what your one- time offer (OTO) will be. Remember, this is a paid product, usually within the $10 - $20 range, but that price point can be different depending on your niche and the product.

The product should be related to your free offer, so it should be either on the same topic or a similar topic, something which your subscribers will be interested in. If your subscribers sign-up to receive your free gift on a particular topic, then it would only make sense to offer them more information in the form of a paid product on that same topic since you already know they are interested in it.

Again, this product should be high quality, something which the buyers of will be thankful for purchasing. You can use private label rights (PLR) material to help create this product, but make sure that your OTO contains useful information that the buyers can put to use, otherwise you may run the risk of disappointing your buyers and being forced to refund many of them.

<u>Hit this blue line to apply.</u>

You will need to create a sales page to offer this OTO along with a download page, both of which can be created using OptimizePress with WordPress.

Within your autoresponder account, which we will talk about later in this report, you will want to set the opt-in form redirect option to automatically send subscribers to this OTO as soon as they submit the sign-up form. When a visitor comes to your squeeze page, if they sign up to your list, they will then be immediately taken to view your one- time offer.

Down-Sell Offer:

The down-sell offer can either be on a slightly different topic as your OTO, or it could be a smaller version of your OTO, either way it should be cheaper in price than your OTO.

This offer is to capture more buyers who did not purchase your OTO but who still want to purchase something from you. Without this down-sell page you will lose out on a lot of sales.

This offer will also need a sales page and a download page.

When visitors are viewing your one-time offer but decide to pass it up, you will want to capture their attention using an exit pop script which displays when they try to close the page to tell them about your down-sell offer. If they decide to stay on the page to view the offer they will be redirected to your down-sell sales page.

At this point you now have all of the web pages needed to start building your list and making money from new subscribers. The next step is to set-up your autoresponder in order to properly capture and keep those subscribers.

<u>Hit this blue line to apply.</u>

Step #2: Autoresponder Set-Up

In order to actually build an email list properly you will need an autoresponder account, and I would suggest one of two autoresponder services to use, Aweber or GetResponse. Those are both professional autoresponder services which I have used and would recommend.

Once you have account and have created your first list within the account, there are a few things which you will need to set-up in order to make the most out of your new list. The first would be to make sure that within your list settings you set the opt-in settings to "single opt-in", not double opt-in. Single opt-in will allow visitors to enter their email address and become subscribed to your list immediately, while double opt-in will force your visitors to have to check their email inbox to confirm signing up to your list, which will dramatically lower the number of subscribers that you will receive.

The second task to do within your new list is to create at least 5 follow-up emails which will start being send automatically to new subscribers as soon as they subscribe. The first email should be a welcome email, thanking the person for subscribing and containing a link to your free gift. You may also want to promote your one-time offer within this email as well, to remind them about it.

The second – fifth emails should be a combination of quality content as well as promotions for your OTO and possibly other products of yours or affiliate products.

The follow-up emails should be set-up to be sent almost every day, with a missed day every 2-3 days. The point of these follow-up emails is to maintain regular contact with your subscribers and to keep building up trust with them, offering them great free content with a few promotions in between.

The more that your subscribers like and trust you, the more likely they will feel comfortable buying from you in the future.

Once your list settings and follow-up emails are in place, you can then create an opt-in form and place it on your squeeze page. Make sure to set it to only have an email field and to redirect subscribers to your one-time offer page.

Now that you have your web pages, your free offer, and your autoresponder set-up, it's time to start sending traffic to build your list up to 1,000 subscribers!

<u>Hit this blue line to apply.</u>

Step #3: Traffic Generation

Traffic is the most important step to this whole system, make sure to focus most of your efforts on this part. You can have the best looking squeeze page with amazing follow-up emails, but if no one visits your squeeze page, then all of that means nothing.

A word of caution: don't get too preoccupied with getting your pages and emails perfect, they can all be edited and changed later. It's important to just get something online and functioning, then start getting traffic and focus on conversion rates later. That's not to say that you should put up ugly pages, but don't spend all of your time trying to perfect them yet.

With that said, here are four great ways to start getting traffic to your squeeze pages, in order of how easy and how quickly they can work.

Solo Ads:

Before I go into detail about solo ads I first want to say that you can find a lot of poor solo ad providers, people who are just in it to make a few bucks. They don't care about their lists or the quality of the traffic they send you. But you can also find a lot of fantastic providers, people who do honestly care about delivering top-notch traffic. Solo ads over the years have gotten a bad name, but they still can work wonders, you just have to be a little more careful now with who you purchase them from.

With that said, solo ads continue to be my first choice for quick traffic and gaining subscribers fast.

In case you are not aware, a solo ad is when someone with an existing list is selling a certain number of clicks (usually 50, 100, 200, 300, etc.) from their list. For example, I can purchase 100 clicks from solo ad provider "Bob" for $40. I will tell Bob what link I want him to promote, which is usually my squeeze page. Bob will then email his list and tell his subscribers about my site. When a subscriber of his clicks to go to my site, that counts as one of the 100 clicks that I purchased.

So how can you build your list up to 1,000 subscribers using solo ads? Simple math will tell you how many solo ad clicks you will need to purchase.

<u>Hit this blue line to apply.</u>

Looking back at the 40% conversion rate I mentioned earlier, if I purchased 100 clicks from Bob, I would end up with 40 new subscribers on my list. So if I kept purchasing 100 click solo ads, I would need to purchase 25 solo ads in order to get 1,000 subscribers on my list.

It's important to understand that you are not forced to only purchase 100 click solo ads. If you have found a good solo ad provider, you can ask them if they are able to deliver more than 100 clicks. If so, you can purchase more, which would cut down on the total number of solo ads that you will need.

But for starters, I would only purchase 50 or 100 clicks from solo ad providers which I haven't bought from in the past. Then if I find that they send quality traffic (if my conversion rates are staying high with their traffic), I may then purchase higher number of clicks from them.

But it is also important to note that the more you promote your squeeze page, no matter how unique it originally was, it will soon lose some of its "newness", you will need to keep testing and changing it up to keep your conversion rates higher. The more you promote it, the more people will see it, which means the more people will by-pass it.

When purchasing a solo ad, you may also want to consider sending the provider a pre- written email that they can send to their list. For the most part, solo ad providers will write their own email to send to their list, but it's often a good idea to send them something anyways so that they can quickly understand what your page is about, allowing them to easily write their own email.

Once you understand all of the above about solo ads, you can now go out and find solo ad providers. There are three main places where I look for providers within the internet marketing niche. The first would be the Warrior Forum under the Classified Ads section. What's great about this is that you can see real reviews of previous buyers, which makes it a lot easier to spot a good seller.

The other two places would be Skype and Facebook groups. These two are a bit harder to find, as they often require you to have been invited to the groups. But once you have purchased a few solo ads from the Warrior Forum, you will then start seeing and hearing about these other places, and you can ask sellers or other buyers where they look and if they can invite you into any groups.

<u>Hit this blue line to apply.</u>

But when you are looking for solo ad sellers there are a few things to be aware of.First would be to learn how they built their list. Anyone can go out today and download thousands of email addresses, but if those email addresses where not legally added to their autoresponder account by the person behind the email address, then that would be illegal to do. Make sure that anyone you purchase from has built up their list one email address at a time, having people opt-in to their list.

Second, make sure that most of their subscribers are from tier 1 countries, United States, Canada, Europe, and Australia. These are the most valuable subscribers, they will be more likely to purchase form you in the future.

Third, make sure that you can see reviews from other buyers. If the solo ad seller is new, that doesn't necessarily mean that their traffic won't be great, but it does mean that you will want to be a bit more cautious. Often you can ask for a lower price if they cannot provide many reviews for you to see.

Fourth, check to see if they will be sending your link to some of their buyers on their list as well. If you can have it sent to buyers, those subscribers are worth a lot more than non-buying subscribers. It may cost you more to send to them, but consider doing so as those subscribers have proven that they are capable of purchasing products.

If the solo ad provider does not freely give out the above information, you should ask them for it. Message them politely to confirm the information. If anything seems suspicious, don't purchase from them.

The last thing to understand is that prices for solo ads will vary. You can find 100 click solo ads for $30, but you can also find them for $70. If a solo ad seller provides quality traffic and has repeat customers, they will probably raise their rates, so don't discount a seller just because they may seem expensive. Although the upfront cost might be higher, you may end up with a lot more one-time offer sales.

I mentioned that I like purchasing solo ads because they can deliver quick traffic, and that's the truth! You see, you don't have to purchase one solo ad and then sit back and wait for it to be delivered until you purchase another solo ad. You can purchase as many as you want, as fast as you want. The only time limit may be at the beginning when you are testing solo ad providers, otherwise, you can quite easily build your list to 1,000 subscribers within a week if you wanted to.

Hit this blue line to apply.

Solo Ad Swaps:

This section is all about free solo ads, getting a solo ad for no-cost because once you have about 500 subscribers you will be able to start sending clicks to other people in exchange for them sending clicks to you.

Following basically the same ideas as purchasing a solo ad, you will want to seek out solo ad swap partners who are willing to send clicks to your squeeze page at the same time you send clicks to their squeeze page.

Like I mentioned, you will need a list of at least 500 subscribers to do this, to be able to send clicks, but once you are able to send at least 50 clicks, then you can start swapping clicks. At first you will not be able to receive a lot of clicks because you will be unable to send many clicks, but over time your list will grow and you will begin to be able to send more and more clicks, resulting in being able to receive more and more clicks.

This is a great way to build up your list at the same time as you are buying solo ads. You can swap and buy solo ads at the same time, not with the same solo ad provider, but with multiple providers.

You can find solo ad swap partners the same way you would a regular solo ad, but mostly through Facebook and Skype groups. Once you have successfully delivered a few swaps, ask your swap partner who else they would recommend to you to swap with.

This is the quickest and best way to get more swap partners.

However, once you start sending solo ad swaps to your emails list you will need to take care to make sure that what you are promoting to your list is not only relevant to your list, but that it also contains good content. Before you send a solo ad swap email, make sure to sign up on your partners squeeze page to test it out. There will be times when you notice that maybe their pages are broken, or maybe they are promoting a product which you do not like. These things can only be noticed if you join their list.

Whatever you send to your list, whether that's a solo ad swap email, pure content email, or your own promotional email, make sure that it contains good content and the link in the email takes your subscribers to good honest pages that will actually help them. Maintaining a good relationship with your list is critical to your long-term success.

Hit this blue line to apply.

Solo ads and solo ad swaps can bring you in a lot of subscribers, so make sure to consider using them from the start. But now let's get into a few other methods.

Free WSO:

If your niche is within the internet marketing niche, then pay attention to this section here. "WSO" stands for Warrior Special Offer, which is a promotional area within the Warrior Forum. Products listed here are geared towards internet marketers, and with the Warrior Forum being one of the top internet marketing forums, this is a great place to advertise your products.

For a listing fee of $40, you can put publish a WSO.

Similar to a solo ad (which on average costs $40 per 100 clicks), you may see similar results with posting a WSO, but you may also see a lot greater results as well. But due to the WSO being in a forum where posts move down the page and onto the next page according to how many new posts there are, you can't be guaranteed any number of clicks or sales/sign-ups. Sometimes you may see a few results, while other times you can see massive results.

99% of WSO's are paid products, usually lower priced at about $10. So what I am suggesting you do is to post a FREE WSO, don't charge for it.

Since most are paid, having something there for free can gain a lot of attention because it's different. One thing to always keep in mind in marketing is to try to be different, stand out from the crowd. Posting a WSO that is not going to cost anyone money to get is being unique.

The product you post will need to be 100% your own, nothing re-worked or that you may have resell rights to. All WSO's need to be your own creation. Because of that I understand that it may take some extra time to put something together, but trust me, it never hurts to have something totally your own. Even after the WSO is posted, you can re-use the product wherever and however you want to.

If your free gift that you are using for your squeeze page is your own creation, consider using that. Otherwise, spend a few hours creating something yourself. It can be a simple

Hit this blue line to apply.

PDF report, videos, graphics, or anything that is on a hot topic. The more that people are talking about a subject, the hotter it is, the better results you will see from you. Look around the forum to see what other people are talking about, see what questions are being asked. Then do a little research to find the answers and create a simple product about that.

You will then need to write a sales letter for the product on the WSO thread. This will entice viewers to want your product. If you write the sales letter the same way you would write it for a paid product, the better chances of the viewer's seeing that and assuming it is a paid product. Imagine what their reaction will be when at the bottom of the sales letter they discover that it's free!

The next step will be to redirect the download button to your squeeze page for them to opt-in to. You may need to create a new squeeze page for this as your original one may not suit the free WSO that well. But again, that's why I like using OptimizePress with WordPress, as it's super easy to create a new squeeze page.

Once they opt-in to the list, redirect them to the download page for that product, and also send them some follow-up emails as mentioned earlier.

What about your one-time offer? Well, you can use one for this too. You can either replace the redirect download page with an offer, or you can use your first follow-up email to tell them about the OTO. You can even use other WSO's that you become an affiliate for to use as the OTO. Either way, you will want to still use an OTO to help offset the cost of posting the WSO itself.

But here's something slightly different that I want to mention. This free WSO method will build you a list, just like the other methods will. But, what if you charged a small amount of money for your WSO product instead of giving it away for free? I'm not talking about charging the same price as a normal product would be charged at, but something small, for example $1 - $5.

Why would you want to do this? Building an email list of buyers is a lot more valuable than a list of subscribers who have not yet proven that they are able to purchase something. By offering your product for a very low cost you will be building a list of subscribers who are capable of spending money online, at the same time as not turning many people away because of a higher price point.

<u>Hit this blue line to apply.</u>

It's up to you how you want to market your WSO. But for the purposes of this report, to get 1,000 subscribers quickly, I would stick to offering your WSO for free, then using the low cost method in the future to start building a list of buyers.

Other List Building Methods:

The above methods are what can bring you the most subscribers in the least amount of time, but there are still other ways that you can build a list, so I wanted to still mention them.

List building methods that use blogging, social media (Facebook, Twitter), and YouTube videos, are fantastic ways to help supplement your overall list building, but they are not the quickest ways to go about list.

You can build a big list using a blog to attract traffic, having your opt-in form on the side of your blog. But the problem with blogging to build a list is that you need to spend time to build up traffic to your blog. It will most likely take several months before you can start seeing a significant amount of traffic, therefore it will take even longer to build up a nice size email list.

Facebook and videos are similar. You can build email lists with them, but you will not see immediate results. You will need to first build up a following in Facebook and YouTube and then redirect visitors to your squeeze page to add them to your list.

What I would recommend would be to use these other methods to help build your list in the long-term, don't do it for quick results or else you will be disappointed. Realize that your overall marketing efforts should contain these other methods (and others too) for the most impact in the coming months and years, but if you are trying to build your list to 1,000 subscribers quickly, then focus on the first mentioned methods.

<u>Hit this blue line to apply.</u>

Take Action!

So there you have it, tried and tested, proven methods to build your list to 1,000 subscribers. The set-up may take some time, but remember not to focus so much on that part that you fail to start building your list. Get your pages and opt-in form set-up, then start list building, don't worry about getting it all perfect yet, you can always edit your pages later.

Once you start, use as many of the methods as you can at the same time for the most results in the quickest time.

Take action; don't wait any longer to start building your list!

Just hit this blue line and confirm your application

Contents